SWU-800- 005

UNIFORMS OF RUSSIAN ARMY DURING THE YEARS 1825-1855 VOL. 5

UNDER THE REIGN OF NICHOLAS I
EMPEROR OF RUSSIA BETWEEN 1825 TO 1855
ENGINEERS, GENERAL STAFF, GARRISON & OTHERS

From the Viskovatov's greatest work:
"Historical description of the clothing and
arms of the Russian Army"

English translation by Mark Conrad

SOLDIERSHOP PUBLISHING

AUTHOR

Aleksandr Vasilevich Viskovatov born 22 April (4 May New Style) 1804, died 27 February (11 March) 1858 in St. Petersburg, Russian military historian. He graduated from the 1st Cadet Corps and served in the artillery, the hydrographic depot of the Naval Ministry, and then in the Department of Military Educational Institutions. He mainly studied historical artifacts and the histories of military units. Viskovatov's greatest work was the Historical Description of the Clothing and Arms of the Russian Army.

Title: **UNIFORMS OF RUSSIAN ARMY DURING THE YEARS 1825-1855. VOL. 5** -Under the reign of Nicholas I emperor of Russia between 1825-1855
By A.V.Viskovatov. Serie edit by Luca S. Cristini. First edition by Soldiershop. January 2019
Cover & Art Design: Luca S. Cristini. Plates re-colorations by Anna Cristini. ISBN code: 978-88-93274067
Published by Luca Cristini Editore, via Orio 35/4- 24050 Zanica (BG) ITALY. www.soldiershop.com

UNIFORMS
OF THE RUSSIAN ARMY
DURING THE YEARS
1825-1855
VOL. 5

UNDER THE REIGN OF NICHOLAS I EMPEROUR OF
RUSSIA BETWEEN 1825 AND 1855

*

ENGINEERS, GENERAL STAFF, GARRISON AND OTHERS

Nicholas I of Russia by Franz Krüger

HISTORICAL DESCRIPTION OF THE CLOTHING AND ARMS
OF THE RUSSIAN ARMY - A.V. VISKOVATOV
(First English translation by Mark Conrad)

Soldiershop is glad to presents the complete collection of the great job made by A.V. Viskovatov dedicated to the uniforms and weapons belonging from the first Zar and Russian emperors to the Russian army during the Napoleonic period, until 1860 about. The time we considered in this volume corresponds to the reigns of Nicholas I that was the Emperor of Russia from 1825 until 1855. He was also the King of Poland and Grand Duke of Finland. He is best known as a political conservative whose reign was marked by geographical expansion, repression of dissent, economic stagnation, poor administrative policies, a corrupt bureaucracy, and frequent wars that culminated in Russia's defeat in the Crimean War of 1853–56.

Our reprint in based on the original 19th century volumes. This part is distributed at now on six volumes.

Our new edition, the first ever published in English, both on paper and digital format, boasts a large number of color plates, many of them unpublished and re-coloured by our team of expert artists and scholars of uniformology. Each volume is based on 100 color plates or more, always accompanied by the original translated text which describes the subjets of the plates.

A unique work in its genre, a must have in any respecting collection!

Aleksandr Vasilevich Viskovatov born 22 April (4 May New Style) 1804, died 27 February (11 March) 1858 in St. Petersburg, Russian military historian. He graduated from the 1st Cadet Corps and served in the artillery, the hydrographic depot of the Naval Ministry, and then in the Department of Military Educational Institutions. He mainly studied historical artifacts and the histories of military units. Viskovatov's greatest work was the Historical Description of the Clothing and Arms of the Russian Army (Vols. 1-30, St. Petersburg, 1841-62; 2nd ed. Vols. 1-34, St. Petersburg - Novosibirsk - Leningrad, 1899-1948). This work is based on a great quantity of archival documents and contains four thousand colored illustrations.

Viskovatov was the author of Chronicles of the Russian Army (Books 1-20, St. Petersburg, 1834-42) and Chronicles of the Russian Imperial Army (Parts 1-7, St. Petersburg, 1852). He collected valuable material on the history of the Russian navy which went into A Short Overview of Russian Naval Campaigns and General Voyages to the End of the XVII Century (St. Petersburg, 1864; 2nd edition Moscow, 1946). Together with A.I. Mikhailovskii-Danilevskii he helped prepare and create the Military Gallery in the Winter Palace. He wrote the historical military inscriptions for the walls of the Hall of St. George in the Great Palace of the Kremlin. (From the article in the Soviet Military Encyclopedia.)

CONTENTS

*

HISTORICAL DESCRIPTION OF THE CLOTHING AND ARMS OF THE RUSSIAN ARMY

Engineers, General Staff, Corps of Topographers, Garrison Regiments and Battalions, Line Battalions, Battalions of the Internal Guard 1825-1855

CHANGES IN THE UNIFORMS AND EQUIPMENT OF TEMPORARY FORCES FROM 1801 TO 1825.

17 - ENGINEERS: FIELD, MARINE CONSTRUCTION SECTION, MILITARY SETTLEMENTS, AND ENGINEER COMMANDS (*U INZHENEROV: POLEVYKH, MORSKOI STROITEL'NOI CHASTI, VOENNYKH POSELENII I V INZHENERNYKH KOMANDAKH*).

11 February 1826 - Field-engineer officers, in place of their previous dark-green pants with high boots and grey riding-trousers with stripes are given long dark-green **pants** with red piping on the side seams. Conductors (*konduktory*, i.e. officer candidates in training, holding non-commissioned officer status and distinctions - M.C.), instead of pants with knee gaiters (*kragi*), are ordered to have the same long **pants** as for officers and black **half-gaiters** (*polushtiblety*) with tin buttons, while the horizontal belt for the knapsack is to be fitted so that it is between the two lower buttons of the coat (Illus. 472) [1].

26 July 1826 - Officers, during the summer, when officers in troop units are in summer pants with gaiters, are ordered to likewise wear **summer pants**, of the pattern established on 11 February for dark-green pants (Illus. 473) [2].

18 August 1826 - Officers, when performing inspections on work outside the capitals, are ordered to be in **half-uniform** (*poluforma*), i.e. in frock coat (*syurtuk*) with epaulettes, without a sword, and wearing the forage cap [3].

15 September 1826 - Conductors (*konduktory*) who have served out the regulation number of years for promotion to officer rank but decline it are ordered to wear a **gold galloon chevron** (*nashivka iz zolotnago galuna*) on the left sleeve above and in addition to the yellow tape chevron (*nashivka iz zheltago basona*) prescribed on 29 March 1825 [4].

1 January 1827 - Officers' epaulettes are to have little forged or stamped **stars** (*kovannyya zvezdochki*) **as rank distinctions**, of the same form and according to the same scheme as described above for Army Infantry and Cavalry [5].

27 February 1827 - Officers and conductors, instead of dark-green **cuff flaps** with red piping, are to have them completely red (Illus. 474) [6].

13 May 1827 - Engineer officers and conductors of the Marine Construction Section are to be distinguished from Field Engineer officers and conductors by white cloth **piping** on the coat's cuff flaps and around the upper edge of the forage cap (Illus. 475) [7].

14 December 1827 - The **chevrons** established on 15 September 1826 for the left sleeves of conductors are ordered to be silver, of the same pattern as the galloon on the collar and cuffs of the coat [8].

24 March 1828 - The **coats** of conductors are not to be tailored with cinches (*peretyazhki*) [9].

24 April 1828 - The following changes were made in articles of uniform and accouterments of conductors in Field as well as Marine Construction units:

1) A new model **shako** (*kiver*) is introduced, identical to that intruduced at this time for non-commissioned officers in the Army Infantry, but with a red pompon and, as before, with a single-flame grenade (Illus. 476.)

2) The **sword-belt** (*portupeya*) is prescribed to be 2 vershoks (3 1/2 inches) wide; the **shoulder belts for the knapsack** (*rantsevye plechevye remni*) — 1 1/2 vershoks (2 5/8 inches); and the **belt across the chest** (*nagrudnyi remen*) — 1 1/8 vershoks (2 inches).

3) **Knapsacks** (*rantsy*) are to be of calfskin (*telyachaya kozha*) as before but with the addition of black leather trim (Illus. 476). [10].

18 May 1829 - Engineer conductors who have been recommended by higher command for promotion to officer rank by virtue of years of service are permitted to have **silver sword knots** (*serebryanye temlyaki*) [11].

10 August 1829 - Conductors in the Georgia Engineer District (*Gruzinskii Inzhenernyi Okrug*) are ordered wear **sheepskin headdresses** (*ovchinnyya shapki*) in place of the shako (*kiver*), of the pattern introduced at this time for Infantry regiments of the Caucasus Corps [12].

29 November 1829 - Conductors are ordered to have the same **sword knots** as in Sapper and Pioneer battalions (Illus. 477) [13].

16 December 1829 - The black **cuffs of officers' frock coats** for both Field Engineers as well as Engineers in the Marine Construction Section are changed to dark green as before, with red piping [14].

24 December 1829 - Field Engineer conductors are ordered to have **shako plates** of the same pattern as for Grenadier Sapper battalions, i.e. on a shield—two crossed axes and a single-flame grenade. Conductors of the Marine Construction Section are prescribed the same plates but with just the grenade and without the axes (Illus. 478) [15].

26 December 1829 - All Engineer officers and conductors are directed to have the **buttons** on their coats, frock coats, and greatcoats made with the raised image of a single-flame grenade [16].

4 April 1831 - Officers and conductors of the newly established **Corps of Engineers for Military Settlements** are prescribed the same uniforms as for Field Engineers, except that cuff flaps on the coat are ordered to be not red, but light green with red piping (Illus. 479 and 480), and the shako badge is to be a single-flame grenade without axes [17].

8 June 1832 - Officers are permitted to wear **moustaches** [18].

3 January 1833 - Cloth **half-gaiters** (*polushtiblety*) and **sword knots** are abolished for conductors (Illus. 481). The latter are to be worn only by those conductors who, based on the above directive of 18 May 1829, have them in silver [19].

20 February 1833 - Conductors are given new pattern **summer pants** (*pantalony*) or **breeches** (*bryuki*), without buttons or integral spats (*kozyrki*) (Illus. 482) [20].

28 March 1834 - A new pattern **short sword** (*tesak*) is confirmed by HIGHEST AUTHORITY, with yellow brass fittings and a straight blade, identical to that introduced at this time for Army Foot Artillery and Sapper battalions [21].

26 September 1834 - Conductors are directed to wear the **knapsack** on two belts lying crosswise over the chest (Illus. 483) [22].

31 January 1836 - Conductors' **greatcoats** (*shineli*) are to have nine buttons instead of ten: six along the front opening, two on the shoulder straps, and one on the flap behind [23].

27 April 1836 - **Pompons** are to be lined with black leather [24].

15 July 1837 - A new pattern of **sash** (*sharf*) is confirmed, identical to that introduced at this time for regiments of Army Infantry and Cavalry and described above [25].

17 December 1837 - A new pattern for officers' **epaulettes** is confirmed, identical to that introduced at this time for regiments of Army Infantry and Cavalry, i.e. with the addition of a fourth twist of braid [26].

4 January 1839 - Officers are not to have any bows or bands (*banty*) on the front of their **pants** or **trousers**. These are to be worn completely smooth in the manner prescribed for lower ranks [27].

16 March 1839 - Conductors' **sword-belts** (*portupei*) are to be 1 1/2 vershoks (2 5/8 inches) wide [28].

16 October 1840 - Conductors who have declined promotion to officer rank and are receiving two-thirds of an ensign's pay are given **silver galloon chevrons** (*shevrony ili nashivki, iz serebryanago galuna*) on the left sleeve of the coat, and adding one more such chevron for every five additional years of service [29].

23 January 1841 - The capes (*bolshie vorotniki*) of officers' **greatcoats** are to be 1 arshin (28 inches) long as measured from the lower edge of the collar (*malyi vorotnik*) [30].

8 April 1843 - Conductors are given a new model **shako** (*kiver*), 4 3/4 vershoks (8 1/3 inches) high and curving slightly inward toward the bottom, as prescribed at this same time for Army Infantry troops (Illus. 484) [31].

2 June 1843 - The **shako plate** is ordered to be fitted so that its lower edge lies at a point halfway across the width of the lacquered shako strap [32].

2 January 1844 - Officers are to have a **cockade** (*kokarda*) on the band of their forage caps, identical to that introduced at this time in regiments of Army Infantry and Cavalry, and described above (Illus. 485) [33].

8 May 1844 - Conductors' shakos (*kivera*) be replaced by **helmets** (*kaski*), of the same pattern as established at this time for the 1st, 2nd, and 3rd Sapper Battalions, i.e. without a plume. The plate on these helmets remains the same as they were on the shakos. (Illus. 486) [34].

2 February 1846 - Company and field-grade Field Engineer officers are to have **helmets** in place of hats, with a plate as for the Grenadier Sapper Battalion and with a white plume instead of black (Illus. 487). Company and field-grade officers of the Corps of Engineers for Military Settlements and the Marine Construction Section are prescribed the same helmets but with a grenadier-pattern plate (Illus. 488), while generals of all three administrations are to have a plate of the pattern for Army Infantry regiments with a gilt crown in the plate's shield (Illus. 489) [35].

9 January 1848 - On those days when they are obliged to remain in ceremonial dress (*prazdnichnaya forma*) after the mounting of the guard (*posle razvoda*), generals and field and company-grade officers are permitted to wear the **frock coat** with helmet and plume for walking-out [36].

24 November 1848, 25 November 1849 - Engineer commands of the **Separate Caucasus Corps** are prescribed the uniforms and equipment laid down on 8 August, 23 September, 31 October, and 24 November 1848, and 25 November 1849, as describe above in detail for Grenadier regiments [37].

13 October 1849- Generals (when in engineer uniform) and field and company-grade officers, instead of rapiers (*shpagi*), are ordered to wear infantry **half-sabers** (*pekhotnyya polusabli*) (Illus. 490) [38].

15 February 1850 - Engineer generals and field and company-grade officers of the **Separate Caucasus Corps**, both Field Engineers and Engineers for Military Settlements, are prescribed the same uniforms and armament as ordered for this corps' troops on 8 August 1848 and described above in detail for Grenadier regiments, but with the appropriate differences in colors and trim and also the following alterations:

a.) The top of the **headdress** has silver galloon with two narrow stripes down the center in the same color as the collar .

b.) On the **parade half-caftan** the collar, cuffs, and cuff flaps are as they were on the former coat; piping on the collar, cuffs, down the front of the half-caftan to the bottom of the skirt, and on the pocket flaps, is of red cloth (Illus. 491).

c.) The **vice-half-caftan** is similar to the half-caftan except that there are no button loops on the collar nor flaps on the cuffs, and only piped cuffs are prescribed: red piping for Field Engineers, light green for Engineers of Military Settlements (Illus. 492) [39].

10 January 1852 - In Engineer commands, **knapsacks with straps, water flasks,** and **greatcoat cases with straps** are abolished [41].

29 April 1854 - Generals and field and company-grade officers are to have, in wartime, **campaign greatcoats** (*pokhodnyya shineli*) of the same color and pattern as the lower ranks' greatcoats, as described above for Grenadier regiments, and applying the same guidelines [40].

18 - GENERAL STAFF (*GENERAL'NYI SHTAB*).

11 February 1826 - For officers of HIS IMPERIAL MAJESTY'S Suite for Quartermaster Affairs (*Svita EGO IMPERATORSKAGO VELICHESTAVA po Kvartirmeisterskoi chasti*), their former pants with high boots and riding trousers with wide stripes are replaced by long dark-green **pants** with red piping down the side seams (Illus. 493) [42].

26 July 1826 - For officers of HIS IMPERIAL MAJESTY'S Suite for Quartermaster Affairs, in summertime when officers in troop units are in summer pants with gaiters, it is ordered that they likewise wear **summer pants**, of the style established on 11 February for dark-green ones (Illus. 494) [43].

18 August 1826 - Officers, when on survey work outside the capitals, are ordered to be in half-uniform (*poluforma*), which is to say in **frock coat** (*syurtuk*) with epaulettes, without a sword, and wearing the forage cap [44].

1 January 1827 - Officers' epaulettes are to have little forged and stamped **stars as rank distinctions** in the same form and scheme as described above for Army Infantry and Cavalry [45].

26 December 1829 - Officers of the General Staff are directed to have the **buttons** on their coats, frock coats, and greatcoats made with the raised image of a single-flame grenade [46].

4 October 1830 - Officers (guards and army) who have completed studies in the Military Academy and are attached (*prichislennyi*) to the General Staff are, while they are with the Staff, ordered to wear when performing duties an **aiguilette** (*aksel'bant*) on their regimental coats and frock coats, of the same color as the buttons [47].

February 1831 - Officers of the General Staff are permitted to wear while on campaign the **half-sabers** introduced on 20 August 1830 for officers of Army Infantry and described above in detail for Grenadier regiments [48].

9 May 1831 - Officers of the General Staff in the **6th Infantry Corps** (previously the Separate Lithuania Corps) are ordered to have the same uniform as other officers of the General Staff, i.e. with red piping and cuff flaps instead of raspberry [49].

8 June 1832 - Officers are permitted to wear **moustaches** [50].

15 July 1837 - Approval is given to the new pattern of officers' **sash**, identical to that introduced at this time for regiments of Army Infantry and Cavalry and described above [51].

17 December 1837 - Approval is given to a new pattern of officers' **epaulettes**, identical to those introduced at this time for regiments of Army Infantry and Cavalry, i.e. with the addition of a fourth twist of braid [52].

4 January 1839 - There are not to be any bows or bands on the fronts of **pants** or **trousers**. These are to be worn completely plain in the manner prescribed for lower ranks [53].

23 January 1841- The capes (*bolshie vorotniki*) of officers' **greatcoats** are to be 1 arshin (28 inches) long as measured from the lower edge of the collar (*malyi vorotnik*) [54].

2 January 1844 - Officers are to have a **cockade** on their forage cap, identical to that introduced at this time for regiments of Army Infantry and Cavalry and described above (Illus. 495) [55].

7 December 1844 - When not on duty, generals who are wearing the uniform coat prescribed for the General Staff, are to have a white plume (*sultan*) on the **hat** (*shlyapa*) instead of a black one, and while on duty they are to wear a **helmet** similar to that introduced on 9 May of this year for Grenadier regiments, but with silver mountings and a white plume (Illus. 496). The same helmet is prescribed for field and company-grade officers, upon which their hats are discontinued [56].

4 January 1845 - Officers' **helmets** are to have, on the right side under the chin-scales, a cockade, as described above for Grenadier and other regiments of Army Infantry (Illus. 497) [58].

14 September 1849 - The **percussion pistol** model for officers is confirmed as described above for Grenadier regiments [59].

13 October 1849 - Generals (when in the uniform of the General Staff) and field and company-grade officers are ordered to have infantry **half-sabers** instead of rapiers [60].

15 February 1851 - Generals and field and company-grade officers in the **Separate Caucasus Corps** are prescribed the same uniforms and armaments as troops of this corps were ordered to have on 8 August 1848 and described above in detail for Grenadier regiments, but with appropriate distinctions in colors and trim, and also the following differences:

a.) The top of the **headdress** has silver galloon with two narrow stripes down the center in the same color as the collar .

b.) On the **parade half-caftan** the collar, cuffs, and cuff flaps are as they were on the former coat; piping on the collar, cuffs, down the front of the half-caftan to the bottom of the skirt, and on the pocket flaps, is of red cloth.

c.) The **vice-half-caftan** is similar to the half-caftan except that no embroidery is authorized on the collar and cuff flaps, only cuffs of dark-green cloth with red piping [61].

18 February 1854 - The regulation laid down on 15 November 1853 for packing **light-cavalry saddlery** and described above in the section for Army Cuirassier regiments is extended to the General Staff [62].

29 April 1854 - Generals and field and company-grade officers of the General Staff are to have campaign **greatcoats** in wartime, of the same pattern as established at this time for Army and Guards troops, and in accordance with the guidance set forth above for Grenadier and Army Cuirassier regiments, but with black velvet collars and shoulder straps, piped red [63].

19 - CORPS OF TOPOGRAPHERS (*KORPUS TOPOGRAFOV*).

11 February 1826 - In place of their previous pants with high boots and riding-trousers with stripes officers are given long dark-green **pants** with light-green piping on the side seams. (Illus. 498) [64].

26 July 1826 - Officers of the Corps of Topographers, during the summer, when officers in troop units are in summer pants with gaiters, are ordered to likewise wear **summer pants**, of the pattern established on 11 February for dark-green pants (Illus. 499) [65].

18 August 1826 - Officers, when performing survey work outside the capitals, are ordered to be in **half-uniform** (*poluforma*), i.e. in frock coat (*syurtuk*) with epaulettes, without a sword, and wearing the forage cap [66].

1 January 1827 - Officers' epaulettes are to have little forged or stamped **stars** (*kovannyya zvezdochki*) **as rank distinctions**, of the same form and according to the same scheme as described above for Army Infantry and Cavalry [67].

24 April 1828 - Topographers are given new **shakos**, identical to those prescribed at this time for non-commmissioned officers in the infantry, but with white fittings and a red pompon, and with a single-flame grenade on the shield of the shako plate (Illus. 500). [68].

18 May 1829 - Topographers who have been recommended by higher command for promotion to officer rank by virtue of years of service are permitted to wear **silver sword knots** (*serebryanye temlyaki*) [69].

26 December 1829 - Officers and topographers are ordered to have the **buttons** on their coats, frock coats, and greatcoats made with the raised image of a single-flame grenade [70].

4 April 1830 - Topographers are ordered to have **wide stripes** (*lampasy*) only on chakchiry (hussar style breeches - M.C.) and dark-green pants, while on the grey riding trousers prescribed for while on campaign, there is to be only a single line of piping [71].

12 April 1832 - Commanders of **topographer companies** are ordered to wear the uniform prescribed for officers of the Corps of Topographers [72].

19 May 1832 - Commanders of **topographer comp.** are prescribed the **standard army uniform** (*obshchii armeiskii mundir*) [73].

8 June 1832 - Officers are permitted to wear **moustaches** [74].

27 January 1835 - Commanders of topographer companies, instead of the standard army uniform currently worn, are ordered to have a uniform similar to that prescribed for officers of the Corps of Topographers, but without embroidery or aiguilette, and with cross-straps for the epaulettes of black cloth and not velvet. Buttons for the Military Topographical Depot's company (*rota Voenno-Topograficheskii Depo*) are to have a single-flame grenade, while buttons in other companies are to have the number assigned to the company, with this also being applied to lower ranks. The commander of the Military Topographical Depot's company is authorized the shako and hat, but commanders of other companies have only the shako, with the same plate as for lower ranks, i.e. with a grenade on the shield. All are prescribed officers' infantry-pattern half-sabers and boots without spurs (Illus. 501) [75].

27 April 1836 - Topographers' **shako pompons** are to be lined with black leather [76].

15 July 1837 - A new pattern of **officers' sash** (*sharf*) is confirmed, identical to that introduced at this time for regiments of Army Infantry and Cavalry and described above [77].

17 December 1837 - A new pattern for **officers' epaulettes** is confirmed, identical to that introduced at this time for regiments of Army Infantry and Cavalry, i.e. with the addition of a fourth twist of braid [78].

4 January 1839 - Officers are not to have any bows or bands (*banty*) on the front of their **pants** or **trousers**. These are to be worn completely smooth in the manner prescribed for lower ranks [79].

16 October 1840 - Topographers who have declined promotion to officer rank and are receiving two-thirds of an ensign's pay are given **silver galloon chevrons** on the left sleeve of the coat, adding one more such chevron for every five additional years of service [80].

23 January 1841 - The capes (*bolshie vorotniki*) of officers' **greatcoats** are to be 1 arshin (28 inches) long as measured from the lower edge of the collar (*malyi vorotnik*) [80].

8 April 1843 - Officers of the Corps of Topographers who in their work are required to be **mounted** are directed to have a mouthpiece (*mundshtuk*), saddle, and shabrack like those prescribed for General-Staff officers, with the only difference being blue (*svetlosinnii*) piping instead of red on the shabrack and pistol holster covers, following the color of the coat piping (Illus. 502). On this same date company commanders and topographers are given a new model **shako** (*kiver*), 4 3/4 vershoks (8 1/3 inches) high and curving slightly inward toward the bottom, as prescribed at this same time for Army Infantry troops (Illus. 502 and 503) [82].

2 June 1843 - The **shako plate** is ordered to be fitted so that its lower edge lies at a point halfway across the width of the lacquered shako strap [83].

2 January 1844 - Officers are to have a **cockade** (*kokarda*) on the band of their forage caps, identical to that introduced at this time in regiments of Army Infantry and Cavalry, and described above (Illus. 504) [84].

3 March 1844 - Topographers are ordered to have:

1.) Pouch (*lyadunka*) with a brass three-flame grenade, in the center of which are the Cyrillic letters *G. Sh.* for the Military Topographical Depot's company, and for other companies—the corresponding number (Illus. 505).

2.) In place the previous pattern saber, the new-pattern **dragoon saber**, but without the bayonet scabbard.

3.) A **crossbelt** over the coat, for the pouch—and

4.) Over the waistbelt, to cover it, a cloth **girdle** (*kushak*) of the pattern for lancers, of two dark-green stripes and one blue (*svetlosinii*) stripe, with blue piping along the edges.

Items to be placed in the **pouch** are the following: hand-held surveying compass (*ruchnaya busol'*) with sighting tube; hand-held plane-table (*menzula*), with handle and dioptric ruler (*dioptrennaya lineika*), and accompanied by a brass scale (*masshtab*) with protractor (*transportir*); small box containing: 6 paints, a piece of solid ink (*tush'*), saucer, two brushes, and a screwdriver for a drawing compass (*tsirkul'*); leather case containing: drawing compass, drawing pen (*reisfeder*), pen knife, two pencils, handle for the brushes, and a piece of gum elastic (*gumielastik*); two wooden drawing squares (*ugol'niki*), wooden ruler, and several sheets of paper for the plane-table [85].

11 October 1844 - Topographers are ordered to have **plumes** on their helmets, as well as **saddlecloths** (*val'trapy*) of the pattern for Dragoons [86].

7 December 1844 - When not on duty, generals who are wearing the uniform coat prescribed for the Corps of Topographers, are to have a white **plume** (*sultan*) on the hat (*shlyapa*) instead of a black one, and while on duty they are to wear a helmet similar to that introduced at this time for the General Staff. The same **helmet** is given to field and company-grade officers of the Corps of Topographers (Illus. 506) as well as to topographers, but the latter have a black hair plume instead of white (Illus. 507). Furthermore, hats are discontinued for all field and company-grade officers [87].

4 January 1845 - The **helmets** of generals and field and company-grade officers are to have, on the right side, a cockade, as described above for the General Staff at this time [88].

18 January 1845 - Commanders of topographer companies and all officers wearing the uniform of the Corps of Topographers are prescribed **helmets** with a white hair plume, following the pattern of the helmets introduced on 7 December 1844 and 4 January 1845 and referred to above (Illsu. 508) [89].

2 September 1846 - The School for Caucasian Surveyors (*shkola Kavkazskikh mezhevshchikov*), reestablished at Topographer Company No. 3 in the Separate Caucasus Corps, is ordered to have clothing of the patterns for topographers, but instead of the dress coat, a *kazakin* coat (like a beshmet, but not quilted - M.C.) of dark-green cloth, without shoulder straps, along with pants of the same color without leather cuffs, grey cloth greatcoats without shoulder straps, and grey riding trousers [90].

16 December 1847 - The **quarter-company**, established for geodesic work in eastern Siberia and attached to the 2nd half-company of **Topographer Company No. 4**, is ordered to have the number 4 on its shoulder straps and pouches [91].

9 January 1848 - On those days when they are obliged to remain in ceremonial dress (*prazdnichnaya forma*) after the mounting of the guard (*posle razvoda*), field and company-grade officers are permitted to wear the **frock coat** for walking out, with helmet and plume [92].

13 October 1849 - Field and company-grade officers of the Corps of Topographers, instead of rapiers (*shpagi*), are ordered to have infantry **half-sabers** (*pekhotnyya polusabli*) [93].

15 February 1850 - Field and company-grade officers of the Corps of Topographers in the **Separate Caucasus Corps** are prescribed the same uniforms and armament as ordered for this corps' troops on 8 August 1848 and described above in detail for Grenadier regiments, but with the appropriate differences in colors and trim and also the following alterations:
a.) The top of the **headdress** has silver galloon with two narrow stripes down the center in the same color as the collar .
b.) On the **parade half-caftan** the collar, cuffs, and cuff flaps are as they were on the former coat; piping on the collar, cuffs, down the front of the half-caftan to the bottom of the skirt, and on the pocket flaps, is of blue (*svetlosinii*) cloth (Illus. 509) .
c.) The **vice-half-caftan** is similar to the half-caftan except that there is no embroidery on the collar nor flaps on the cuffs, and there is only a dark-green cloth cuff with blue piping [94].

4 March 1851 - The **half-company** of Topographers established to survey government lands in eastern Siberia is ordered to have the number 4 on its shoulder straps [95].

20 - GARRISON REGIMENTS AND BATTALIONS (*GARNIZONNYE POLKI I BATALIONY*).

11 February 1826 - Officers and lower combatant ranks of Garrison regiments and battalions are given **single-breasted coats** instead of double-breasted, with nine flat buttons in front, dark-green cuff flaps, and red piping down the front opening, from the bottom front to the skirts, and, for officers, also on the pocket folds (*karmannye skladki*) (Illus 510, 511 and 512). (*Note: red cuffs and collars - M.C.*)
The former officers' grey riding-trousers and white pants with high boots and the lower ranks' same white pants but with knee gaiters are replaced with long, dark-green **pants** with red piping on the side seams. Lower ranks at all times, and company-grade officers only in formation, wear black cloth **half-gaiters** under these pants and over the boots, fastened with five or six small brass buttons. Along with this change, the horizontal **belt for the knapsack** is to be between the two lower buttons on the front of the coat, while the **greatcoat** is carried on the knapsack rolled into a tube in its special oilskin case made of raven's-duck [96].

15 September 1826 - Lower ranks who have completed the regulation number of years of faultless service and voluntarily remain on active duty are to wear, above the yellow tape chevrons on the left sleeve established on 29 March 1825, an additional gold **galloon chevron** (*nashivka iz zolotago galuna*) [97].

1 January 1827 - Officers' epaulettes are to have little forged and stamped stars as **rank distinctions**, regardless of the number already thereon, in the same form and scheme as set forth above for Grenadier and other Army infantry regiments [98].

14 December 1827 - The **chevron** to be sewn on the left sleeve, established for lower ranks on 15 September 1826, is ordered to be silver instead of gold [99].

24 March 1828 - The **coats** of lower ranks are not to be tailored with cinches [100].

24 April 1828 - 24 April 1828 - The following changes were made in items of uniform and accouterments:
1) A new model **shako** (*kiver*) is introduced, 5 1/2 vershoks (9 5/8 inches) high with a top diameter not less than 5 5/8 vershoks (9 7/8 inches) and not more than 6 vershoks (10 1/2 inches). The lower diameter will be the size of the head. The

thickness of the upper, lacquered edge is 5/16 vershok (1/2 inch). (Illus. 513 and 514.)

2) The **shako badge** (*gerb*) is ordered to of white tin, depicting a three-flame grenade, and on this is cut out the number of the regiment or battalion (Illus 513 and 514).

3) The **pouch belt** (*perevyaz*) and **sword-belt** (*portupeya*) are prescribed to be 2 vershoks (3 1/2 inches) wide; the **shoulder belts for the knapsack** (*rantsevye plechevye remni*) — 1 1/2 vershok (2 5/8 inches); and the **belt across the chest** (*nagrudnyi remen*) — 1 1/8 vershok (2 inches).

4) **Knapsacks** are to be of calfskin (*telyachaya kozha*) as before but with black leather trim. The knapsack is prescribed to be 9 vershoks (15 3/4 inches) broad, 8 vershoks (14 inches) high, and 2 vershoks (4 3/8 inches) wide. The length of the cover from the upper edge is 6 vershoks (10 1/2 inches).

5) In place of their grey coats (*mundiry*), all **non-combatant non-commissioned officers** are issued with dark-green **frock coats** (*syurtuki*) with a single row of buttons and the same collar, cuffs, and shoulder straps as for combatant personnel. **Pants**, however, are grey with red piping on the side seams.

6.) **Non-combatant craftsmen** (*masterovye*) of the lower ranks, as well as medical orderlies (*lazaretnye sluzhiteli*) are to replace their coats with grey cloth **jackets** (*kurtki*) modeled on the coat, while pants are to be as for the non-combatants above [101].

21 - LINE BATTALIONS (*LINEINYE BATALIONY*).

19 April 1829 - The eight *Caucasus*, fifteen *Orenburg*, and fifteen *Siberian* **Line battalions**, formed from the garrison regiments and battalions of the Separate Caucasus Corps as well as those stationed in the Orenburg territory and Siberia, are ordered to keep their previous uniforms, being distinguished only by the colored cloth on epaulettes and shoulder straps. These colors were designated: for Caucasus battalions — white, without letter or number; for Orenburg battalions — blue (*svetlosinii*), with the yellow numeral 26 signifying the divisional number; for the Siberian battalions — dark green, with red piping and a yellow numeral 27. All all these battalions it is ordered that there be small grenades on the shako with a cut-out number signifying the battalion (Illus. 515 and 516) [102].

10 August 1829 - In Caucasus Line battalions the shako is replaced by a **sheepskin headdress** (*shapka*), identical to that introduced at this time for Grenadier, Carabineer, Infantry, and Jäger regiments of the Separate Caucaus Corps (Illus. 517) [103].

2 October 1829 - All **Line battalions** are ordered to have:

   a) Red collars.

   b) Dark-green cuff flaps on the coat, with red piping.

   c) Tinned buttons on the cloth half-gaiters (*polushtiblety*).

   d) Crossbelts, waistbelts, knapsacks, musket straps, straps for the greatcoat and mess tin, and frizzen covers (*ognivnye chekhly*) — of white Russian leather, of the patterns for Jäger regiments, blackened with black polish.

   e) On the pouch covers there are to be brass numbers following the style for Jäger regiments, the same as prescribed for the shako grenades.

Other items of uniform and armaments remain unchanged (Illus. 517) [104].

16 December 1829 - The cuffs of officers' **frock coats** (*syurtuki*) are ordered to be dark green with red piping [105].

18 January 1830 - The newly established twelve **Georgia Line battalions** in the Separate Caucasus Corps are prescribed the same uniform as Caucasus Line battalions [106].

20 August 1830 - Officers' rapiers (*shpagi*) are replaced with **half-sabers** (*polusabli*) of the same pattern as established at this time for Grenadier and other Army infantry regiments (Illus. 518) [107].

31 October 1830 - Lower ranks of **Orenburg Line Battalions Nos. 2 and 3**, which up to 19 April 1829 formed the Orenburg Garrison Regiment, are ordered to keep their previous shako cords they had since 13 December 1824, but of the new pattern established on 24 April 1828 for Grenadier and other regiments (Illus. 519) [108].

14 February 1831 - With the changes in the numbering of certain divisions, **Orenburg Line battalions** are ordered to have the number 28 on epaulettes and shoulder straps, and **Siberia Line battalions** — 29 [109].

8 June 1832 - Officers are permitted to wear **moustaches** [110].

3 January 1833 - Cloth **half-gaiters** (*polushtiblety*) are abolished for company-grade officers and lower ranks. **Sword knots** are abolished for non-commissioned officers, musicians, and drummers, as are **covers** for shakos and cartridge pouches for non-commissioned officers and privates (Illus. 520) [111].

20 January 1833 - **Covers** for shakos are restored as before [112].

20 February 1833 - All combatant ranks are given new-pattern **summer pants** or **breeches** (*pantalony ili bryuki*), without buttons or integral spats (Illus. 521) [113].

22 February 1833 - Field and company-grade officers are ordered not to use the hat, but rather wear the **shako** at all times [114].

29 January 1834 - In order to introduce uniformity to **shako chin straps**, it is ordered that they be of black Russian leather, 1/2 vershok (7/8 inch) wide, sewn to the left side of the shako underneath the lower reinforcement strap, flush, and fastened by a button sewn onto the right side of the shako above the lower reinforcement [115].

15 March 1834 - With the division of **Line battalions of the Caucasus Corps** into 16 Georgia, 10 Black Sea, and 11 Caucasus, shoulder straps for the first are ordered to be red with a yellow battalion number and a yellow Cyrillic letter G.; in the second — white with a red number and likewise red Cyrillic Ch.; and in the third — blue (*svetlosinii*) with a yellow number and likewise yellow letter K. [116].

19 May 1834 - With the general changes in the numbering of Infantry divisions, the epaulettes and shoulder straps in **Orenburg Line battalions** are ordered to have the number 22, and in the Siberian battalions — 23 [117].

26 September 1834 - Lower ranks are directed to wear the **knapsack** on two belts lying crosswise over the chest (Illus. 522) [118].

3 July 1835 - The newly formed 12 **Finland Line battalions** are prescribed the same uniform as Orenburg and Siberian Line battalions, along with they are to have dark-green shoulder straps with red piping and a yellow number 21 [119].

20 August 1835 - It is ordered that:

1) Officers wear the **knapsack** using only two shoulder belts, without any cross strap or chest strap. These belts are to be lacquered.

2) For lower ranks a **linen case** (*kholshchevyi chekhol*) or pocket (*karman*) for the forage cap is to be put on the outside of the knapsack on the side that lies on the soldier's back. These cases are to be made from the linings of wornout coats.

3) For drummers the **knapsack** is to have one belt as before, worn over the left shoulder [120].

31 January 1836 - The lower ranks' **greatcoat** (*shinel*) is to have nine buttons instead of ten: six along the front opening, two on the shoulder straps, and one on the flap behind [121].

2 February 1836 - Officers of **Finland Line battalions** are ordered to have **gorgets**. These are to be identical to those prescribed for Grenadier and other Army infantry regiments (Illus. 523) [122].

15 March 1836 - For all Line battalions **forage caps** are ordered to be a single pattern: dark green, with a red cloth band and piping, and with the company number on the band, of yellow cloth [123].

27 April 1836 - The lower **pompons** (*repeiki*) are to be lined with black leather [124].

14 January 1837 - Handles of **entrenching tools** are to have the wooden parts varnished, and the same directives for the fitting and carrying of these tools apply as described above for Grenadier regiments [125].

15 July 1837 - Confirmation is given to the new pattern of officers' **sash**, identical to that introduced at this time for Army infantry regiments and described above for Grenadier regiments [126].

17 December 1837 - Confirmation is given to a new pattern of officers' **epaulettes**, identical to those introduced at this time, and described above, for Grenadier regiments [127].

4 January 1839 - Field and company-grade officers are not to have any bows or bands on the front of their **pants** or **trousers**. These are to be worn completely plain in the manner prescribed for lower ranks [128].

16 March 1839 - Lower ranks' **pouch-belts** and **sword-belts** (*perevyazi i portupei*) are to be 1 1/2 vershoks (2 3/5 inches)wide, while **drummers' crossbelts** are as before, 2 1/2 vershoks (4 2/5 inches) wide [129].

16 October 1840 - Lower combatant ranks who voluntarily remain in service after completing the regulation period for retirement are to be given sewn-on **chevrons of silver galloon** to be worn on the left sleeve, one every five years that are served [130].

23 January 1841- The capes (*bolshie vorotniki*) of officers' **greatcoats** are to be 28 inches long as measured from the lower edge of the collar (*malyi vorotnik*) [131].

19 March 1841- Sword belts (*portupei*) are taken away from privates, and it is directed that they only have **crossbelts** (*perevyazi*) with a frog for the bayonet that in full parade dress (*polnaya paradnaya forma*) is buttoned to the pouch and worn over the left shoulder, while in half-dress (*poluforma*), when personnel are without pouches, it is worn over the right shoulder (Illus. 524) [132].

26 November 1842 - Until a new uniform is approved, officers and lower combatant ranks of the Georgia, Black-Sea, and Caucasus Line battalions, are to wear **forage caps** in place of the sheepskin headdress (Illus. 524 and 525) [133].

16 January 1843 - To distinguish lower ranks who have committed transgressions and undergone punishments from other personnel serving without fault, thin **sewn-on cords** (*nashivki iz tonkago snurka*) are established, to be worn across the shoulder straps on dress coats and greatcoats below any numbers or letters:

1.) For those who have attempted two desertions—of grey cord, in two rows; for three desertions—in three rows, and so on, with the addition of one row for each desertion.

2.) For those punished by running the gauntlet (*nakazannye shpitsrutenami*), not for desertion but for some other transgression—of black cord: one cord for each time the man was run through the formation [134].

21 February 1843 - The aforementioned grey and black **cords** are ordered to be sewn onto the shoulder straps of greatcoats as well as dress coats, below the cut-out number [135].

8 April 1843 - Officers and lower ranks of the Finland, Orenburg, and Siberian Line battalions are given a new pattern **shako**, 4 3/4 vershoks (8 1/3 inches) high and curving slightly inward toward the bottom (Illus. 526). Along with this, trim on the shoulder straps (*nashivki na plechevye pogony*) of sergeants (*feldfebeli*), non-commissioned officers (*unter-ofitsery*), and lance-corporals (*yefreitory*) is established following the same scheme as for these ranks in Grenadier and other regiments [136].

10 May 1843 - The covers of the **cartridge-pouches** (*patronnyya sumki*) are not to have any break on top (*bez pereloma vverkhu*), and are to measure (with the cover sewn onto the body of the pouch): length — 5 vershoks (8 3/4 inches), width at the top edge — 5 1/2 vershoks (9 5/8 inches), width at the bottom edge — 6 vershoks (10 1/2 inches) [137].

2 January 1844 - Officers are to have an oval metallic **cockade** on the front of their forage caps, of the same colors as prescribed for the cockades on officer's hats [138].

9 May 1844 - Officers and lower ranks in Finland, Orenburg, and Siberian Line battalions are given **helmets** in place of shakos, of the same pattern as established at this time for other troops, without plumes, with chinscales and army-pattern plates of white tin, with this last item having the brass letter or numbers prescribed for each battalion (Illus. 527) [139].

4 January 1845 - Officers' **helmets** are to have, on the right side under the chin-scales, a metallic cockade (Illus. 528) [140].

23 June 1846 - Upon the introduction of percussion-lock weapons, a description for fitting the **firing-cap pouch** is approved [141].

8 August 1848 - **Georgia, Black-Sea, and Caucasus Line battalions** are prescribed the new uniform and equipment confirmed at this time for Grenadier regiments and described in detail above (Illus. 529 and 530) [142].

28 April 1849 - Approval is given to a description of the method for wearing the **rolled-up greatcoat** in Line battlions of the Separate Caucasus Corps, laid out above for Sapper battalions [143].

9 and 25 November 1849 - The fitting of **helmets** is confirmed as described in detail above for Grenadier regiments [144].

17 January 1851 - Approval is given to the description of folding up and turning back the skirts of the **greatcoat** as laid out above for Grenadier regiments [145].

8 July 1851 - The **gun-lock covers** (*polunagalishcha*) are abolished and approval given to the patterns and descriptions of the **drum**, **fife case** for Caucasus troops, **water flask**, **greatcoat strap**, **sword-belt**, **crossbelt**, and **cover for the firing nipple** of percussion weapons, all as presented above for Grenadier regiments [146].

20 October 1851 - Approval is given to the list and description of items which the soldier is to carry in his **knapsack**, as presented above for Grenadier regiments [147].

26 January 1852 - Non-combatant lower ranks with grey cloth **forage caps** are to have the cap band in the same color as the collar [148].

3 January 1853 - Non-combatant lower ranks with **frock coats** are to have these reach to the lower part of the knee [149].

29 April 1854 - Field and company-grade officers are to have campaign **greatcoats** in wartime, and company-grade officers a sword belt over the shoulder, in the same pattern and worn according to the same directives as issued at this time for Grenadier regiments [150].

22 - BATTALIONS OF THE INTERNAL GUARD (*BATALIONY VNUTRENNEI STRAZHI*).

11 February 1826 - Lower ranks in battalions of the Internal Guard are given **single-breasted coats** (*mundiry*) instead of double-breasted, grey in color as previously, with yellow collars and cuffs, red piping on the tail turnbacks, and nine flat (*ploskii*) buttons in front. Pants with knee gaiters (*kragi*) are replaced with long **pants** the same color as the coat, with yellow piping on the side seams (Illus. 531). Officers keep their dark-green coats with yellow collar, cuffs, and piping on the pocket flaps; red lining on the turnbacks, and nine buttons in one row down the front. Pants are grey with yellow piping on the side seams (Illus. 532). Lower ranks at all times, and company-grade officers (*ober-ofitsery*) only when in formation, are ordered to wear black cloth **half-gaiters** (*polushtiblety*), fastened with five or six small brass buttons. Along with this change, the horizontal **belt for the knapsack** (*poperechnyi rantsevyi remen*) is to be between the two lower buttons on the front of the coat, while the **greatcoat** (*shinel*) is carried on the knapsack (*ranets*) rolled into a tube in its special oilskin case made of raven's-duck (*ravenduchnaya kleenka*) [151].

15 September 1826- Lower ranks who have completed the regulation number of years of faultless service and voluntarily remain on active duty are to wear a gold **galloon chevron** (*nashivka iz galuna*) on the left sleeve, as related above for Grenadier regiments. [152].

1 January 1827 - Officers' epaulettes, in addition to any number, are to have little gold forged and stamped stars as **rank distinctions** in the same form and scheme as described above for Grenadier and other regiments of Army infantry [153].

14 December 1827 - The **chevrons** for the left sleeve established for lower ranks on 15 September 1826 are ordered to be silver instead of gold [154].

24 March 1828 - The **coats** of lower ranks are not to be tailored with cinches [155].

24 April 1828 - New **shakos** are given, of the same pattern as described above for Garrison regiments and battalions, with the only difference being that in battalions of the Internal Guard the small grenades have a single flame instead of three (Illus. 533) [156].

20 September 1829 - A new allocation of Internal Guard battalions is confirmed, based on which they are prescribed the following **numbers**:

District I: St.-Petersburg Battalion — No. 1; Reval — No. 2; Pskov — No. 3; Mitau — No. 4; Riga — No. 5; Arensburg — No. 6.
District II: Novgorod — No. 7; Tver — No. 8; Yaroslavl' — No. 9; Vladimir — No. 10; Kostrtoma — No. 11; Vologda — No. 12.
District III: Sveaborg — No. 13; Viborg — No. 14; Petrozavodsk — No. 15; 1st Archangel — No. 16; 2nd *ditto* — No. 17; 3rd *ditto* — No. 18.
District IV: Nizhnii-Novgorod — No. 19; 1st Kazan — No. 20; 2nd Kazan — No. 21; Simbirsk — No. 22; Vyatka — No. 23; Perm — No. 24.
District V: Penza — No. 25; Saratov — No. 26; Tambov — No. 27; Voronezh — No. 28; Orel — No. 29; Tula — No. 30.
District VI: Vitebsk — No. 31; Smolensk — No. 32; Mogilev — No. 33; Kaluga — No. 34; Moscow — No. 35; Ryazan — No. 36.
District VII: Zhitomir — No. 37; Kiev — No. 38; Chernigov — No. 39; Poltava — No. 40; Khar'kov — No. 41; Kursk — No. 42.
District VIII: Yekaterinoslav — No. 43; Kherson — No. 44; Taurica — No. 45; Kishinev — No. 46; Kamenets-Podol'sk — No. 47.
District IX: Bialystok — No. 48; Grodno — No. 49; Vilna — No. 50; Minsk — No. 51.

As before, the district number is on the shoulder straps and the battalion number on the shako grenades [157].

2 October 1829 - All battalions of the **Internal Guard** are ordered to have:

  a) Dark-green coat, collar, and cuff flaps; red cuffs, collar piping, piping down the front of the coat and on the cuff flaps and lining on the tails; red shoulder straps with yellow figures.

  b) Dark-green pants with red piping.

  c) Tin buttons on the cloth half-gaiters.

  d) Crossbelt, swordbelt, knapsack straps, musket sling, greatcoat strap, and mess-tin strap, and also frizzen covers of white Russian leather, are all to be of the patterns for Jäger regiments, blackened with black polish.

  e) Brass numbers on the pouch lid, following the pattern for Jäger reg. and the same as prescribed for the shako grenades.

  f) Other items of uniform and armaments remain unchanged (Illus. 534 and 535) [158].

16 December 1829 - The cuffs of officers' **frock coats** (*syurtuki*) are ordered to be dark green with red piping [159].

20 August 1830 - Officers' rapiers (*shpagi*) are replaced with **half-sabers** (*polusabli*) of the same pattern confirmed at this time for Grenadier and other Army infantry regiments [160].

8 May 1832 - The newly formed **Modlin and Zamosc battalions** are prescribed: on epaulettes and shoulder straps—the number 10, and on shako grenades and the covers of cartridge pouches for the Modlin battalion—the number 52, and for the Zamosc—53 [161].

8 June 1832 - Officers are permitted to wear **moustaches** [162].

3 January 1833 - **Cloth half-gaiters** (*polushtiblety*) are abolished for company-grade officers and lower ranks , as are sword knots for non-commissioned officers and drummers. **Covers** for shakos and cartridge pouches are abolished for non-commissioned officers and privates [163].

12 January 1833 - The newly established **Warsaw Garrison Battalion** is ordered to have the number 54 on shakos and pouches, and on epaulettes and shoulder straps—the number 10 [164].

20 January 1833 - **Covers** for shakos are restored as before [165].

20 February 1833 - All combatant ranks are given new pattern **summer pants** or **breeches** (*pantalony ili bryuki*), without buttons or integral spats (Illus. 536) [166].

22 February 1833 - Field and company-grade officers are not to use the hat, but rather wear the **shako** at all times [167].

29 January 1834 - In order to introduce uniformity to shako **chin straps**, it is ordered that they be of black Russian leather, 1/2 vershok (7/8 inch) wide, sewn to the left side of the shako underneath the lower reinforcement strap, flush, and fastened by a button sewn onto the right side of the shako above the lower reinforcement [168].

26 September 1834 - Lower ranks are directed to wear the **knapsack** on two belts lying crosswise over the chest (Illus. 537) [169].

20 August 1835 - A directive regarding officers' **knapsacks** (*rantsy*) is issued , the same as set forth above for Line battalions [170].

31 January 1836 - The lower ranks' **greatcoat** (*shinel*) is to have nine buttons instead of ten: six along the front opening, two on the shoulder straps, and one on the flap behind [171].

27 April 1836 - The lower **pompons** (*repeiki*) are to be lined with black leather [172].

15 July 1837 - Approval is given to the new pattern of officers' **sash**, identical to that introduced at this time for Army infantry regiments and described above for Grenadier regiments [173].

17 December 1837 - Approval is given to a new pattern of officers' **epaulettes**, identical to those introduced at this time for Grenadier regiments and described above [174].

4 January 1839 - Field and company-grade officers are not to have any bows or bands on the front of their **pants** or **trousers**. These are to be worn completely plain in the manner prescribed for lower ranks [175].

19 February 1839 - **Shako covers** are abolished for those battalions on a field establishment (*na polevom polozhenii*): St. Petersburg, Moscow, 1st, 2nd, and 3rd Archangel, and 1st and 2nd Kazan [176].

16 March 1839 - Lower ranks' **pouch-belts** and **sword-belts** (*perevyazi i portupei*) are to be 1 1/2 vershoks (2 3/5 inches)wide, while **drummers' crossbelts** are as before, 2 1/2 vershoks (4 2/5 inches) wide [177].

16 October 1840 - Lower combatant ranks who voluntarily remain in service after serving out the regulation period for retirement are to be given sewn-on silver galloon **chevrons** for the left sleeve, after every five years service [178].

23 January 1841 - The capes (*bolshie vorotniki*) of officers' **greatcoats** are to be 1 arshin (28 inches) long as measured from the lower edge of the collar (*malyi vorotnik*) [179].

19 March 1841 - **Sword belts** (*portupei*) are taken away from privates, and it is directed that they only have **crossbelts** (*perevyazi*) with a frog for the bayonet that in full parade dress (*polnaya paradnaya forma*) is buttoned to the pouch and worn over the left shoulder, while in half-dress (*poluforma*), when personnel are without pouches, it is worn over the right shoulder [180].

16 January 1843 - To distinguish lower ranks who have committed transgressions and undergone punishments **sewn-on grey and black cords** are established, on the same basis as related above for Line battalions [181].

21 February 1843 - The aforementioned grey and black **cords** are ordered to be sewn onto the shoulder straps of greatcoats as well as dress coats, below the cut-out number [182].

8 April 1843 - Officers and lower ranks are given a new pattern **shako**, 4 3/4 vershoks (8 1/3 inches) high and curving slightly inward toward the bottom. Along with this, trim on the shoulder straps (*nashivki na plechevye pogony*) of sergeants (*feldfebeli*), non-commissioned officers (*unter-ofitsery*), and lance-corporals (*yefreitory*) is established following the same scheme as for these ranks in Infantry and Jäger regiments [183].

10 May 1843 - The covers of the **cartridge-pouches** (*patronnyya sumki*) are not to have any break on top (*bez pereloma vverkhu*), and are to measure (with the cover sewn onto the body of the pouch): length — 5 vershoks (8 3/4 inches), width at the top edge — 5 1/2 vershoks (9 5/8 inches), width at the bottom edge — 6 vershoks (10 1/2 inches) [184].

2 January 1844 - Officers are to have a **cockade** on the front of their forage caps, identical to those established at this time for Line battalions [185].

9 May 1844 - Officers and lower ranks are given **helmets** in place of shakos, identical to those confirmed at this time for Line battalions but with a three-flame grenade with the battalion number cut out on it, and, as before, with a black chin strap (*podborodnyi remen'*) for lower ranks (Illus. 538) [186].

4 January 1845 - Officers' **helmets** are to have a cockade on the right side under the chin-scales [187].

30 March 1845 - The St.-Petersburg and Moscow battalions are ordered to have **metal chin-scales** on their helmets instead of chin straps [188].

23 June 1846 - Upon the introduction of percussion-lock weapons, the description for fitting the **firing-cap pouch** is approved as detailed above for Grenadier regiments (Illus. 539) [189].

9 and 25 November 1849 - The fitting of **helmets** is confirmed as described in detail above for Grenadier regiments [190].

17 January 1851 - Approval is given to the descriptions for folding up and turning back the skirts of the **greatcoat** as laid out above for Grenadier regiments [191].

8 July 1851 - **Gun-lock covers** (*polunagalishcha*) are abolished and approval given to the patterns and descriptions of the drum, **water flask**, **greatcoat strap**, **sword-belt**, **crossbelt**, and **cover for the firing nipple** of percussion weapons, all as presented above for Grenadier regiments [192].

26 January 1852 - Non-combatant lower ranks with grey cloth **forage caps** are to have the cap band in the same color as the collar [193].

3 January 1853 - Non-combatant lower ranks authorized **frock coats** are to have these reach to the lower part of the knee [194].

29 April 1854 - Field and company-grade officers of the Novgorod and Tver Internal Garrison Battalions, upon their being made mobile, are to have campaign **greatcoats** in wartime, and company-grade officers a sword belt over the shoulder, of the same patterns as introduced on this date for active forces and described above for Grenadier regiments, but with changes in colors as appropriate for lower ranks of the Internal Guard [195].

Nicholas I of Russia in military winter dress

NOTES

(1) Collection of Laws and Directives, 1826, Book I, pg. 105.
(2) Ibid., Book III, pg. 161.
(3) Ibid., pg. 197.
(4) Ibid., pg. 255.
(5) Ibid., 1827, Book I, pg. 3.
(6) Ibid., pg. 153.
(7) Information received from the Department of the Marine Construction Section.
(8) Collection of Laws and Directives, 1827, Book IV, pg. 257.
(9) Ibid., 1828, Book I, pg. 211.
(10) Ibid., Book II, pp. 131 et seq.
(11) Ibid., 1829, Book II, pg. 221.
(12) Ibid., Book III, pg. 129, and information from the Commissariat Department of the War Ministry.
(13) Collection of Laws and Directives, 1830, Book IV, pg. 445.
(14) Ibid., 1829, Book IV, pg. 107.
(15) Ibid., pg. 223.
(16) Ibid., pg. 115.
(17) Collection of Laws and Directives, 1831, Book II, pg. 112, § 14, and information from the Commissariat Department of the War Ministry.
(18) Ibid., 1832, Book II, pg. 545
(19) Ibid., 1833, Book I, pg. 419.
(20) Ibid., pg. 463.
(21) Information from the Artillery Department of the War Ministry, and HIGHEST Confirmed model for short swords.
(22) Collection of Laws and Directives, 1834, Book III, pg. 465.
(23) Ibid., 1836, Book I, pg. 137.
(24) Information from the Commissariat Department of the War Ministry.
(25) Collection of Laws and Directives, 1837, Book III, pg. 47.
(26) Ibid., Book IV, pg. 325.
(27) Ibid., 1839, Book I, pg. 3.
(28) Ibid., pg. 179.
(29) Order of the Minister of War, 16 October 1840, N° 60.
(30) Ibid., 23 January 1841, N° 8.
(31) Ibid., 8 April 1843, N° N° 46 and 47.
(32) Ibid., 2 June 1843, N° 78.
(33) Ibid., 2 January 1844, N° 1.
(34) Ibid., 9 May 1844, N°N° 63 and 64.
(35) Ibid., 2 February 1846, N° 26.
(36) Ibid., 9 January 1848, N° 8.
(37) Ibid., 24 November 1849, N° 197.
(38) Ibid., 13 October 1849, N° 104.
(39) Ibid., 15 February 1850, N° 13.
(40) Ibid., 29 April 1854, N° 53.
(41) Ibid., 10 January 1852, N° 4.
(42) Collection of Laws and Directives, 1826, Book I, pg. 105, and statements by persons who served in the Quartermaster Section at that time.
(43) Ibid., Book III, pg. 161.
(44) Collection of Laws and Directives, 1826, Book III, pg. 197.
(45) Ibid., 1827, Book I, pg. 3.
(46) Ibid., 1829, Book IV, pg. 115.
(47) HIGHEST Confirmed Regulation for the Military Academy, 4 October 1830, § 46.
(48) Collection of Laws and Directives, 1831, Book I, pg. 58.
(49) Ibid., Book II, pg. 39, and statements by persons who serviced in the General Staff.
(50) Collection of Laws and Directives, 1832, Book II, pg. 545.
(51) Ibid., 1837, Book III, pg. 47.
(52) Ibid., Book IV, pg. 325.
(53) Ibid., 1839, Book I, pg. 3.
(54) Order of the Minister of War, 23 January 1841, N° 8.
(55) Ibid., 2 January 1844, N° 1.
(56) Ibid., 7 December 1844, N° 147.
(57) Ibid., 4 January 1845, N° 1.
(58) Ibid., 9 January 1848, N° 8.

(59) Ibid., 14 September 1849, N° 88.
(60) Ibid., 13 October 1849, N° 104.
(61) Ibid., 15 February 1850, N° 13.
(62) Ibid., 16 October 1840, N° 71.
(63) Ibid., 29 April 1854, N° 53.
(64) Collection of Laws and Directives, 1826, Book I, pg. 105.
(65) Ibid., Book III, pg. 161.
(66) Ibid., pg. 197.
(67) Ibid., 1827, Book I, pg. 3.
(68) Ibid., 1828, Book II, pg. 131 et seq.
(69) Ibid., 1829, Book II, pg. 221.
(70) Ibid., Book IV, pg. 115.
(71) Ibid., 1830, Book II, pg. 95.
(72) Ibid., 1832, Book II, pg. 91.
(73) Ibid., pg. 521.
(74) Ibid., pg. 545.
(75) Ibid., 1835, Book I, pg. 41.
(76) Ibid., 1836, Book II, pg. 171.
(77) Ibid., 1837, Book III, pg. 47.
(78) Ibid., Book IV, pg. 325.
(79) Ibid., 1839, Book I, pg. 3.
(80) Order of the Minister of War, 16 October 1840, N° 71.
(81) Ibid., 23 January 1841, N° 8.
(82) Ibid., 8 April 1841, N° N° 44 and 46.
(83) Ibid., 2 June 1843, N° 78.
(84) Ibid., 2 January 1844, N° 1.
(85) Ibid., 3 March 1844, N° 27.
(86) Ibid., 11 October 1844, N° 124.
(87) Ibid., 7 December 1844, N° 147.
(88) Ibid., 4 January 1845, N° 1.
(89) Ibid., 18 January 1845, N° 11.
(90) Ukase to the Senate, 9 October 1846.
(91) Order of the Minister of War, 16 December 1847, N° 196.
(92) Ibid., 9 January 1848, N° 8.
(93) Ibid., 13 October 1849, N° 104.
(94) Ibid., 15 February 1850, N° 13.
(95) Ibid., 4 March 1851, N° 24.
(96) Collection of Laws and Directives, 1826, Book I, pgs. 105 and 125.
(97) Ibid., Book III, pg. 255.
(98) Ibid., 1827, Book I, pg. 3.
(99) Ibid., Book IV, pg. 257.
(100) Ibid., 1828, Book II, pg. 211.
(101) Ibid., Book II, pg. 131 et seq.
(102) Ibid., pg. 51.
(103) Ibid., Book III, pg. 129, and information from the Commissariat Department of the War Ministry.
(104) Collection of Laws and Directives, 1829, Book IV, pg. 3.
(105) Ibid., pg. 107.
(106) Information from the Commissariat Department of the War Ministry.
(107) Collection of Laws and Directives, 1830, Book III, pg. 179.
(108) Ibid., Book IV, pg. 223.
(109) Ibid., 1831, Book I, pg. 49.
(110) Ibid., 1832, Book II, pg. 545.
(111) Ibid., 1833, Book I, pg. 419.
(112) Ibid., pg. 435.
(113) Ibid., pg. 463.
(114) Ibid., 1833, Book I, pg. 465.
(115) Ibid., 1835, Book I, pg. 197.
(116) Ibid., pg. 95.
(117) Ibid., Book III, pg. 147.
(118) Ibid., Book III, pg. 465.
(119) Ibid., 1835, Book III, pg. 10.

(120) Ibid., pg. 179.
(121) Ibid., 1836, Book I, pg. 137.
(122) Ibid., pg. 37.
(123) Ibid., pg. 147.
(124) Ibid., Book II, pg. 171.
(125) Ibid., 1837, Book I, pg. 353.
(126) Ibid., Book III, pg. 47.
(127) Ibid., Book IV, pg. 325.
(128) Ibid., 1839, Book I, pg. 3.
(129) Ibid., pg. 179.
(130) Order of the Minister of War, 16 October 1840, N° 71.
(131) Ibid., 23 January 1841, N° 8.
(132) Ibid., 19 March 1841, N° 23.
(133) Archive of the Inspection Department of the War Ministry, correspondence for 1842, Sect. 2, 2nd Desk, N° 365.
(134) Order of the Minister of War, 16 January 1843, N° 6.
(135) Ibid., 21 February 1843, N° 24.
(136) Ibid., 8 April 1843, N°N° 46 and 47.
(137) Ibid., 10 May 1843, N° 63.
(138) Ibid., 2 Janurary 1844, N° 1.
(139) Ibid., 9 May 1844, N° 63.
(140) Ibid., 4 January 1845, N° 1.
(141) Ibid., 8 March 1847, N° 46.
(142) Orders of the Minister of War: 8 August, 23 September, 31 October, and 24 November 1848,
(143) Order of the Minister of War, 28 April 1849, N° 34.
(144) Orders of the Minister of War: 9 and 25 November 1849, N°N° 110 and 117.
(145) Order of the Minister of War, 17 January 1851, N° 7.
(146) Ibid., 13 December 1851, N° 7.
(147) Ibid., 20 October 1851, N° 120.
(148) Ibid., 26 January 1852, N° 15.
(149) Ibid., 3 January 1853, N° 3.
(150) Ibid., 29 April 1854, N° 53.
(151) Collection of Laws and Directives, 1826, Book I, pgs. 105 and 125.
(152) Ibid., Book III, pg. 255.
(153) Ibid., 1827, Book I, pg. 3.
(154) Ibid., Book IV, pg. 257.
(155) Ibid., 1828, Book I, pg. 211.
(156) Ibid., Book II, pg. 131 et seq.
(157) Ibid., 1829, Book III, pgs. 321-323.
(158) Ibid., Book IV, pg. 3.
(159) Ibid., pg. 107.
(160) Ibid., 1830, Book III, pg. 179.
(161) Ibid., 1832, Book II, pg. 481.
(162) Ibid., pg. 545.
(163) Ibid., 1833, Book I, pg. 419.
(164) Ibid., pg. 3.
(165) Ibid., pg. 435.
(166) Ibid., pg. 463.
(167) Ibid., pg. 465.
(168) Ibid., 1834, Book I, pg. 197.
(169) Ibid., Book III, pg. 465.
(170) Ibid., 1835, Book III, pg. 179.
(171) Ibid., 1836, Book I, pg. 137.
(172) Ibid., Book II, pg. 171.
(173) Ibid., 1837, Book III, pg. 47.
(174) Ibid., Book IV, pg. 325.
(175) Ibid., 1839, Book I, pg. 3.
(176) Ibid., pg. 171.
(177) Ibid., pg. 179.
(178) Order of the Minister of War, 16 October 1840, N° 71.
(179) Ibid., 23 January 1841, N° 8.
(180) Ibid., 19 March 1841, N° 23.

(181) Ibid., 16 January 1843, N° 6.
(182) Ibid., 21 February 1843, N° 24.
(183) Ibid., 8 April 1843, N°N° 46 and 47.
(184) Ibid., 10 May 1843, N° 63.
(185) Ibid., 2 January 1844, N° 1.
(186) Ibid., 9 May 1844, N° 63.
(187) Ibid., 4 January 1845, N° 1.
(188) Correspondence of HIM Main Staff with the Commander of the Separate Corps of the Internal Guard, 30 March 1845, N° 2885.
(189) Order of the Minister of War, 8 March 1847, N° 46.
(190) Orders of the Minister of War, 9 and 25 November 1849, N°N° 110 and 117.
(191) Order of the Minister of War, 17 January 1851, N° 7.
(192) Ibid., 13 December 1851, N° 134.
(193) Ibid., 26 January 1852, N° 15.
(194) Ibid., 3 January 1853, N° 3.
(195) Ibid., 29 April 1854, N° 53.

РИСУНКИ

ОДЕЖДЫ и ВООРУЖЕНІЯ

РОССІЙСКИХЪ

ВОЙСКЪ

1825-1855.

PLATES LIST OF ILLUSTRATIONS

511. Non-commissioned Officer and Company-grade Officer. Garrison Regiments and Battalions. 1826-1828.

512. Non-commissioned Officer and Private. Garrison Regiments and Battalions. 1826-1829.

513. Private. Garrison Regiments and Battalions. 1828 and 1829.

514. Company-grade Officer. Garrison Regiments and Battalions. 1828 and 1829.

515. Company-grade Officer and Private. Siberian Line Battalions. 1829.

516. Private. Caucasus Line Battalions. 1829.

517. Non-commissioned Officer and Company-grade Officer. Caucasus Line Battalions. 1829-1833. (Note: In 1830 officers' rapiers were replaced by half-sabers.)

518. Company-grade officer. Line Battalions. 1830-1843.

519. Private and Non-commissioned Officer. Orenburg Line Battalions NºNº 2 and 3. 1830-1833.

520. Company-grade Officer and Non-commissioned Officer. Siberian Line Battalions. 1833-1843.

521. Drummer and Company-grade Officer. Orenburg Line Battalions. 1833-1843.

522. Private. Siberian Line Battalions. 1834-1843.

523. Company-grade Officer. Finland Line Battalions. 1836-1843.

524. Privates. Line Battalions of the Separate Caucasus Corps. 1842-1848.

525. Field-grade Officers. Line Battalions of the Separate Caucasus Corps. 1842-1848.

526. Non-commissioned Officer and Company-grade Officer. Orenburg Line Battalions. 1843 and 1844.

527. Company-grade Officer and Drummer. Finland Line Battalions. 1844.

528. Field-grade Officer. Line Battalions. 1845-1855.

529. Privates. Georgia and Black-Sea Line Battalions. 1848-1855.

530. Company-grade Officer. Caucasus Line Battalions. 1848-1855.

531. Non-commissioned Officer and Private. Internal Garrison Battalions. 1826-1828.

532. Company-grade Officer. Internal Garrison Battalions. 1826-1828.

533. Company-grade Officer and Private. Internal Garrison Battalions. 1828 and 1829.

534. Private and Non-commissioned Officer. Internal Garrison Battalions. 1829-1833.

535. Company-grade Officer. Internal Garrison Battalions.1829-1833.

536. Drummer and Company-grade Officer. Internal Garrison Battalions. 1833-1843.

537. Non-commissioned Officer. Internal Garrision Battalions. 1834-1843.

538. Company-grade Officer and Private. Internal Garrison Battalions. 1844.

539. Non-commissioned Officer. St.-Petersburg Internal Garrison Battalion. 1846-1849.

Company-grade Officer of Field Engineers and Conductor. 1826 and 1827.

Company-grade Officer of Field Engineers. 1826 and 1827.

Conductor and Field-grade Officer of Field Engineers. 1827 and 1828.

Engineer Conductor and Company-grade Officer of the Marine Construction Section. 1827 and 1828.

Engineer Conductor and Conductor of the Marine Construction Section. 1828 and 1829.

Engineer Conductor. 1829-1833.

Engineer Conductor and Conductor of the Marine Construction Section. 1829-1833.

General and Field-grade Officer. Corps of Engineers of the Military Settlements. 1831-1846.

Conductor. Corps of Engineers of the Military Settlements. 1831-1843.

Engineer Conductor. 1833-1843.

Engineer Conductor of the Marine Construction Section. 1833-1843.

Engineer Conductor. 1834-1843.

. *Conductor. Corps of Engineers of the Military Settlements. 1843 and 1844.*

Field-Engineer Company-grade Officer and Company-grade Officers of the Marine Construction Section. 1844-1855.

Conductors: Engineers, Military Settlements, and Marine Construction Section. 1844-1849.

Field-Engineer Company-grade Officers. 1846-1849.

Field-grade Officer. Corps of Engineers of the Military Settlements. 1846-1849.

General. Engineers of the Marine Construction Section. 1846-1849.

Company-grade Officer. Engineers of the Marine Construction Section. 1849-1855.

Company-grade Officers. Field Engineer and Engineer of the the Military Settlements, in the Separate Caucasus Corps. 1850-1855.

Company-grade Officers. Field Engineer and Engineer of the Military Settlements, in the Separate Caucasus Corps. 1850-1855.

Company-grade Officer. General Staff. 1826-1844.

Field-grade Officer. General Staff. 1826-1844.

Company-grade Officer. General Staff. 1844-1855.

Generals. General Staff. 1844-1849.

Field-grade Officer. General Staff. 1845-1849.

Company-grade Officer. Corps of Topographers. 1826-1844.

Company-grade Officer. Corps of Topographers. 1826-1844.

Topographer. Corps of Topographers. 1828-1843.

Company-grade Officer. Commander of Topographer Company. 1835-1843. (Note: In the printed volume, this plate erroneously anticipates the title of Plate 535: "Company-grade Officer. Internal Garrison Battalions. 1829-1833." - M.C.)

Company-grade Officers. Corps of Topographers and Commander of Topographer Company. 1843 and 1844.

Topographer. 1843 and 1844.

Field-grade Officer. Corps of Topographers. 1844-1855.

Topographers. 1844.

Company-grade Officer. Corps of Topographer. 1844-1849.

Topographer. 1844-1849.

508

Company-grade Officer. Commander of Topographer Company. 1845-1849.

Company-grade Officer. Corps of Topographers in the Separate Caucasus Corps. 1850-1855.

Private and Drummer. Garrison Regiments and Battalions. 1826-1828.

Non-commissioned Officer and Company-grade Officer. Garrison Regiments and Battalions. 1826-1828.

Non-commissioned Officer and Private. Garrison Regiments and Battalions. 1826-1829.

Private. Garrison Regiments and Battalions. 1828 and 1829.

Company-grade Officer. Garrison Regiments and Battalions. 1828 and 1829.

Company-grade Officer and Private. Siberian Line Battalions. 1829.

516

Private. Caucasus Line Battalions. 1829.

NCO and Company-grade Officer. Caucasus Line Battalions. 1829-1833. (Note: In 1830 officers' rapiers were replaced by half-sabers.)

Company-grade officer. Line Battalions. 1830-1843.

Private and Non-commissioned Officer. Orenburg Line Battalions No No 2 and 3. 1830-1833.

Company-grade Officer and Non-commissioned Officer. Siberian Line Battalions. 1833-1843.

Drummer and Company-grade Officer. Orenburg Line Battalions. 1833-1843.

Private. Siberian Line Battalions. 1834-1843.

Company-grade Officer. Finland Line Battalions. 1836-1843.

Privates. Line Battalions of the Separate Caucasus Corps. 1842-1848.

525

Field-grade Officers. Line Battalions of the Separate Caucasus Corps. 1842-1848.

Non-commissioned Officer and Company-grade Officer. Orenburg Line Battalions. 1843 and 1844.

Company-grade Officer and Drummer. Finland Line Battalions. 1844.

Field-grade Officer. Line Battalions. 1845-1855.

Privates. Georgia and Black-Sea Line Battalions. 1848-1855.

Company-grade Officer. Caucasus Line Battalions. 1848-1855.

Non-commissioned Officer and Private. Internal Garrison Battalions. 1826-1828.

Company-grade Officer. Internal Garrison Battalions. 1826-1828.

Company-grade Officer and Private. Internal Garrison Battalions. 1828 and 1829.

Private and Non-commissioned Officer. Internal Garrison Battalions. 1829-1833.

Company-grade Officer. Internal Garrison Battalions. 1829-1833.

Drummer and Company-grade Officer. Internal Garrison Battalions. 1833-1843.

Non-commissioned Officer. Internal Garrision Battalions. 1834-1843.

Company-grade Officer and Private. Internal Garrison Battalions. 1844.

Non-commissioned Officer. St.-Petersburg Internal Garrison Battalion. 1846-1849.

SOLDIERS, WEAPONS & UNIFORMS ALREADY PUBLISHED
(SOME TITLES)

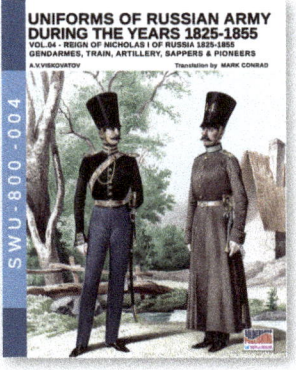
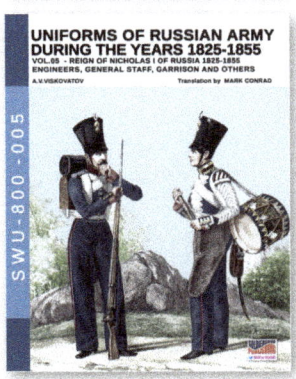

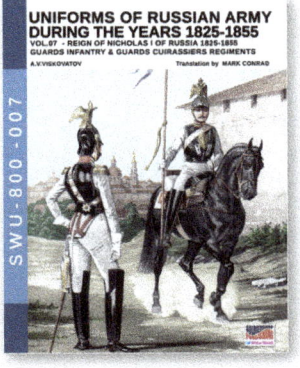

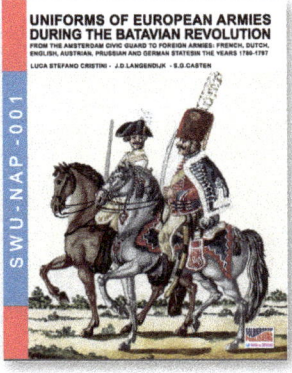

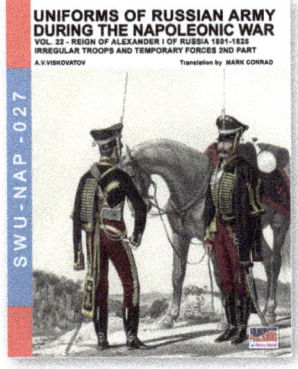
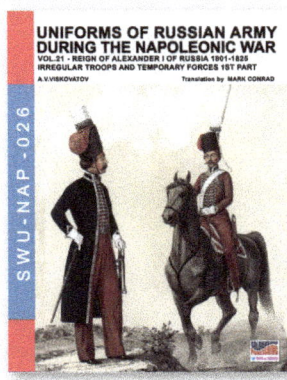

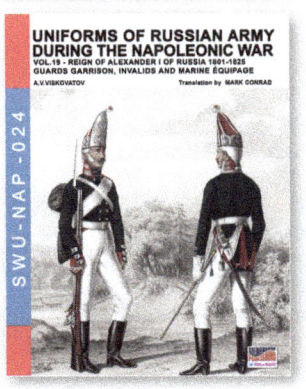

www.ingramcontent.com/pod-product-compliance
Lightning Source LLC
Chambersburg PA
CBHW041148120626
46547CB00020B/3150